The Prisoner's Guide to Filing a Winning Grievance

Larry "Rocky" Harris

Cover photo: Adobe Stock © venerala

ISBN: 978-0-578-52975-2

ACKNOWLEDGEMENTS

The following book was an idea brought to pen and paper by my editor and mentor, Sally Fallon Morell. In our discussions, she planted the seed in my brainpan. From there it grew into this finished product.

A big thanks to Nancy Fields, my webmaster. She took the edited manuscript from page to online format. Her input is much appreciated.

I want to thank my daughter, Amanda Carrasco, for her help in research. For many a day my request for her to walk the information highway—to which I have no access—is met with , "Okay, Dad, I got you!" Without her research, this writer would have been stuck on stupid.

Without these three helpers, I would just be twisting in the wind. As with all my books, this book carries the fingerprints of these ladies all through it. From where I sit incarcerated, I can only say "Thank-you!"

CONTENTS

PREFACE

Under the United States Constitution, every state and federal prisoner has the First Amendment right to complain about his or her conditions of confinement. It is a right not lost by the American citizen while incarcerated in a state of federal prison. This right is a "protected activity" under the First Amendment to the U.S. Constitution.

The complaint is submitted by filing a grievance, also referred to as "exhausting your state remedies required."

When you file a grievance, it is an illegal act for any prison staff, such as guards, counselors or wardens, to retaliate in any way; furthermore, it is illegal to threaten a prisoner in any manner, such as with tickets, placement in segregation, solicited assaults by prisoner or staff, or theft of property. These acts are often done to deter the prisoner from exercising this right, but these acts are illegal. The prisoner can expose these acts in a federal court of law and receive damages.

Throughout this book I will explain the law and give you the case law and citations that support this concept under our great Constitution.

Under the 1996 Prison Litigation Reform Act, several laws were put into place. Under this set of laws, the state prisoner is now required to exhaust his or her state remedies before he or she may seek a federal review on any constitutional violation claim.

Since I am a prisoner in the State of Illinois, I will focus on conditions in my state throughout this booklet. However, the processes that I am describing here will generally apply to every state.

In the State of Illinois, when filing a grievance, each prisoner must complete the three steps required by the Illinois Department of Corrections (IDOC). Before you can file for relief in a federal court, the grievance procedure must be completed and copies of all three steps attached to your civil right complaint. All three steps must be completed. See Federal Statute 42 U.S.C. § 1983 at U.S.C § 1997 (e)(a): "No action shall be brought with respect to prison conditions under [42 U.S.C. § 1983]…or any other federal law by a prisoner confined in any jail, prison, or other correctional facility until such administrative remedies as are available are exhausted."

This legal hurdle was put in place to trip the prisoner up. It allows the Attorney General's Office in Illinois (or in any state) to cite a technical violation and get your civil rights complaint dismissed because you did not get the three steps completed first. Remember, if you make this mistake you will still be charged the filing fee. After you have filed your grievance form with your counselor, every grievance filed will require:

1. The Counselor's response. If the Counselor does not correct the problem, then you submit the grievance form to the Grievance Officer and Chief Administrative Officer's (CAO). (The CAO is the top warden.)

2. The Grievance Officer and Chief Administrative Officer's (CAO) response. If the CAO does not correct the problem, then you submit your grievence form, along with the responses to The Administrative

Review Board. The address of the Board should be on the form. In Illinois, the address is

Illinois Administrative Review Board
IDOC Center
P. O. Box 19277
Springfield, Illinois 62794-9277

3. The Administrative Review Board's response.

If the Board's response is negative, then you may file for redress in a state or federal court, having completed all three steps. Be sure to make copies of the original grievance and every response.

In this book I will explain the game for you, giving you the rules and the law. I will explain things in simple terms. Unfortunately, our ignorance of the law is often used to do us wrong. It is only fair when both sides know the rules in which this chess match is played.

America is truly a great country. As an American citizen you retain your constitutional rights—the rights guaranteed to you by the U.S. Constitution's Bill of Rights—even when you are a prisoner. The prison administrators often look at us as just a bunch of dumb thugs too inept and lazy to play this legal game and win. They plan to beat you on a mistake, a technicality you missed, and have your claim dismissed. Then they can rake you under the carpet in silence. However, as a prisoner in a state or federal facility you retain these rights.

Remember this if nothing else: you live in a house of law; the prison administrators work in a house of law. In America, neither side is above the law. Learn the law and change will come from the courts, for a prisoner can win in the man's arena if he knows how to play the game.

CHAPTER ONE
THE GRIEVANCE PROCEDURE

The grievance procedure in Illinois is a three-step process that each state prisoner must complete. It has time limits for filing and receiving your answer. It is set up to give the state employee the chance to resolve the issue at the state level. This "Exhaustion of State Remedies" must be completed before you may seek a federal or state court review on the claim.

The law is cut and dry here. There is no way to beat the system in place. One very smart Attorney General once said, "The prisoner is too lazy to do the paperwork. A large percentage of the State prisoner lawsuits will stop. We will not settle anymore. For the 1996 Prison Litigation Act has given us the tools to dismiss their case before the claim is even heard." As long as the prisoner does not know the rules, she is right.

So you must adhere to the rules of the game. Now there are several avenues to completing this grievance. It depends largely on the issue being grieved by the prisoner. So let us set down the basic steps here first. In the Illinois Department of Corrections, these are the three steps:

1. State your grievance verbally to the counselor. If not resolved, file the grievance form with your counselor.

2. If not resolved with the counselor, submit your grievance form to the Grievance Officer & Chief Administrative Officer's response. The Chief Administrative Officer (CAO) is the head warden at any prison. This warden will sign your grievance.

3. If not resolved with the Chief Administrative Officer, then submit your grievance to:

   Illinois Administrative Review Board
   IDOC Center
   P. O. Box 19277
   Springfield, Illinois 62794-9277

Here is the law delivered by the U.S. Federal Judge S.C. Williams, of the U.S. Southern District of Illinois. In the case of *Harris-vs-Schwartz, 3:10-cv-00596-MJR-SCW* at Document #44, the Judge issued this following opinion on the Illinois State Grievance procedure. "As an inmate confined within the Illinois Department of Corrections, plaintiff was required to follow the regulations contained in the Illinois Department of Correction's Grievance Procedures for Offenders ("grievance procedure") to properly exhaust his claims. (20 Ill. Administrative Code § 504.800 et seg.) The grievance procedure first requires inmates to speak with the counselor about his complaint. (20 Ill. Admin Code § 504.810(a).) Then, if the counselor does not resolve the issue, the inmate must file a grievance form directed to the grievance officer within 60 days of the incident being grieved. The grievance form must: "contain factual details regarding each aspect of the offender's complaint, including what happened, when, where, and the name of each person who is subject of or who is otherwise involved in the complaint. The provision does not preclude an offender from filing a grievance when the names of the individuals are not known, but the offender must include as much descriptive information about the individual as possible. (So on most grievance issues it must start by talking with a counselor, and then the grievance form being sent to the counselor for a response.)

Judge Williams then continues: (20 Ill. Admin. Code § 504.810 (a)(b).) The Grievance Officer shall [then] consider the grievance and report his or her findings and recommendation in writing to the Chief Administrative Officer [who] shall advise the offender of the decision in writing within 2 months after receipt of the written grievance, where reasonably feasible under the circumstances." (20 Ill. Admin. Code § 504.830 (d).) If the inmate is not satisfied with the Chief Administrative Officer's response, he or she can file an appeal with the Director through the Administrative Review Board (A.R.B.). The grievance procedures specifically state, "[i]f after receiving the response of the Chief Administrative Officer, the offender still feels that the problem, complaint or grievance has not been resolved to his or her satisfaction, he or she may appeal in writing to the director within 30 days after the date of the decision. Copies of the Grievance Officer's report and the Chief Administrative Officer's decision should be attached. (20 Ill. Admin. Code § 504.850 (a).)"

"The Administrative Review Board shall submit to the Director a written report of its findings and recommendations." (20 Ill. Admin. Code § 504.850(e).). The Director shall review the findings and recommendations of the Board and make a final determination of the grievance within 6 months after receipt of the appealed grievance, where reasonably feasible under the circumstances. The offender shall be sent a copy of the Director's decision. (20 Ill. Admin. Code § 504.840 (a).) If an inmate forwards the grievance to the CAO as an emergency grievance, then the CAO "shall expedite processing of the grievance and respond to the offender" indicating to him which course he has decided is necessary after reading the grievance. (20 Ill. Admin. Code § 504.840 (b).) Once the CAO has informed the inmate of his decision, the inmate may then appeal that decision to the ARB (Administrative Review Board) on an expedited basis. (20 Ill. Admin. Code § 504.850(g).)"

These are the words of the federal judge in the U.S. Southern District of Illinois, the interpretation of the Illinois Department of Correction grievance procedure. So there is no arguing, no Joe Blow said this or that. This is the law standard. If you do not follow it you will place your actions in jeopardy of being dismissed—these are technicalities to beat you, to make it difficult to get heard and get damages on your claim.

Perhaps your fellow prisoner will tell you there are many ways to bring a claim, many ways to skin that cat; but all state and federal courts require the three steps to be exhausted.

Remember, to keep copies of everything because these copies a must be attached to any petition you file in a federal or state court. If not attached, you will face a Pavey hearing (see Chapter Thirteen).

This is where the paper trail you built will help you prevail. The state attorney general. assigned to your case will argue that you did not complete your grievance procedure. Therefore you case should be dismissed in their favor. See *PAVEY-vs-CONLEY, 544 F. 3d 739, 740-41 (7th Cir. 2008).*

But when you produce the copies of the letters requesting the counselor, the grievance officer, the warden, and the ARB answer your grievance you have flipped the script on them. The State IDOC staff can not deliberately deny you access to court by failing to answer your grievance. See this case for a better read of the law here. This is an unpublished case the state wants to keep hidden but I brought it to light. The Illinois prisoner won at the Pavey hearing. This was an IDOC Taylorville Facility case. J*ohn MORO-vs-Angela WINSOR, 2008 WL 718687 at Case No. 05-cv-452-JPG SD Ill.* March 14th, 2008.

I will get into this fact with deeper case law later in the book. For every prisoner has the right to request this hearing. I strongly suggest you do that once the court sets the date for the "Exhaustion of State Remedies Defense Hearing." For you must argue and protect your case once you have finished the grievances issue. If they did not respond, and kept you from producing the copies of the three steps, this is a required hearing to defend your case.

The law states a prisoner must first try to resolve this issue, the complaint, "in-house" first. This means you try to get the matter addressed and solved through a Sargent, a Lieutenant, or the Counselor. Maybe even bend the warden's ear. But we all know it is a rare thing to happen. So next you must file the grievance to start the process. We all have great rights in the United States. But you must do the paperwork sometimes to get them enforced.

On the next page you will find an example of the Illinois grievance form. filled out with a sample grievance. See how it is filled out; see that it is drafted in language that is simple and to the point. Remember, you have 60 days from the incident to file your grievance. If you miss this time frame you have defaulted. It is over. There will be no further review of the claim. So remember to get it in writing as soon as you can.

Housing Unit: ________ Bed #: ________

ILLINOIS DEPARTMENT OF CORRECTIONS
OFFENDER'S GRIEVANCE

Date:	Offender: (Please Print)	ID#:
Present Facility:	Facility where grievance issue occurred:	

NATURE OF GRIEVANCE:

- ☐ Personal Property
- ☐ Staff Conduct
- ☐ Transfer Denial by Facility
- ☐ Mail Handling
- ☐ Dietary
- ☐ Other (specify): ________
- ☐ Restoration of Good Time
- ☐ Medical Treatment
- ☐ ADA Disability Accommodation
- ☐ HIPAA

☐ Disciplinary Report: ____/____/____ (Date of Report) ________ (Facility where issued)

Note: Protective Custody Denials may be grieved immediately via the local administration on the protective custody status notification.

Complete: Attach a copy of any pertinent document (such as a Disciplinary Report, Shakedown Record, etc.) and send to:

Counselor, unless the issue involves discipline, is deemed an emergency, or is subject to direct review by the Administrative Review Board.
Grievance Officer, only if the issue involves discipline at the present facility or issue not resolved by Counselor.
Chief Administrative Officer, only if **EMERGENCY** grievance.
Administrative Review Board, only if the issue involves protective custody, involuntary administration of psychotropic drugs, issues from another facility except medical and personal property issues, or issues not resolved by the Chief Administrative Officer.

Summary of Grievance (Provide information including a description of what happened, when and where it happened, and the name or identifying information for each person involved): ________

Relief Requested: ________

☐ Check **only** if this is an **EMERGENCY** grievance due to a substantial risk of imminent personal injury or other serious or irreparable harm to self.
☐ Check if this is **NOT** an emergency grievance.

________ Offender's Signature ________ ID# ____/____/____ Date

(Continue on reverse side if necessary)

Counselor's Response (if applicable)

Date Received: ____/____/____

☐ Send directly to Grievance Officer

☐ Outside jurisdiction of this facility. Send to Administrative Review Board, P.O. Box 19277, Springfield, IL 62794-9277

Response: ________

________ Print Counselor's Name ________ Counselor's Signature ____/____/____ Date of Response

EMERGENCY REVIEW

Date Received: ____/____/____

Is this determined to be of an emergency nature?

☐ Yes; expedite emergency grievance
☐ No; an emergency is not substantiated. Offender should submit this grievance in the normal manner.

________ Chief Administrative Officer's Signature ____/____/____ Date

Distribution: Master File; Offender — Page 1 — DOC 0046 (1/2018)

Printed on Recycled Paper

The Counselor has fourteen days to respond to your grievance. After that period of time has gone you must protect your claim. Write a simple letter requesting the counselor respond to your grievance filed, and be sure to make a copy.

SAMPLE REMINDER LETTER

Hello Counselor,

RE: Grievance Mailed 3-10-2015

It is now 3/24/2015. Two weeks have passed since I sent you my grievance. Did you receive it? If not I retain a copy. I can send you another copy to process.

The grievance dealt with an overcharge at the Commissary. A copy of my receipt was attached for your review.

Please let me know you received it. I await your response.

Respectfully,

Johnny Convict

As a prisoner in the IDOC we all know that the gremlins misplace our grievances on a regular basis. There is a reason for this mischief. There is a madness behind this mystery. The timeline for filing the grievance is 60 days from the incident being grieved. So if the dirty deed went down on May 1st,, you have until June 29th to file your grievance. Yes, May contains thirty-one days. Every little mistake is a way to dismiss your claim. A technicality to rake you under the carpet. Just remember that 60 days is 60 days and not necessarily two months!

Remember to make a copy of everything: filled out grievance form , follow-up letter to your counselor requesting an answer, etc. Keep copies of everything all the way up the line. Nobody cares about your beef but you. Do not depend on another here, for you will be sadly disappointed. If the counselor does not respond after 60 days has passed, he may write you off as "Defaulted due to timeline. Did not file the grievance in the 60 day timeframe."

Even though you did file it, you are beat if you don't have the paper trail requesting the grievance be answered. It will be your word against the counselor. You said you filed it, and the Counselor states, "I never receive one." Now whom do you think the Judge will believe here. Thus, the paper trail will tip the scales of justice in your favor when you produce the letters requesting the counselor's answer. See *MORO-vs WINSOR, 2008 WL 718687 Case No. 05-cv-452 JPG SD Ill. March 14th, 2008* on this fact.

WHERE TO FILE

One choice you have on the grievance form is Disciplinary Report. If your grievance is written in protest of a Disciplinary Report (also called a ticket), it goes straight to the grievance officer. There is no need of a counselor's response in this case. Furthermore, if you are transferred on a "Disciplinary Transfer," you need to file this grievance straight to the Administrative Review Board in Springfield because the prison you were transferred from will kill the grievance. They do this hoping you fail to re-file. Then the 60-day time frame rule comes into play. Once the 60 days have passed, and no grievance has been sent to Springfield, you have defaulted. Failure to prosecute your grievance is on you. They win that argument every time. Again, make copies of everything!

On the grievance form you will find instructions that determine your proper grievance procedure.

- Submit to counselor unless the issue involved discipline, is deemed an emergency, or is subject to direct review by the Administrative Review Board.

- Submit directly to grievance officer (the CAO or warden) only if the issue involves discipline at the present facility, is an emergency grievance or an issue not resolved by the counselor.

- Submit directly to the Administrative Review Board only if the issue involves transfer denial by the Transfer Coordinator, protective custody, involuntary administration of psychotropic drugs, issues from another facility except personal property issues, or issues not resolved by the Chief Administrative Officer,

Always remember the time line here. The counselor must get grievance within 60 days of the incident (or the Grievance Officer, or Administrative Review Board when the situation applies).

The counselor has 14 days to respond. Then the grievance form goes straight to Grievance Officer. He has 60 days to reply.

When you get the Grievance Officer's report, sign at the bottom. You have 30 days to mail out the grievance to the Administrative Review Board if you want to appeal the decision given by the Grievance Officer, and agreed to by the Warden. Remember, you have thirty days from the date the Warden, (Chief Administrative Officer) signed off on it.

WRITING THE CORRECT GRIEVANCE

Judge Williams lay down the law. In his opinion he stated the requirements on the grievance. We live in a house of law. The prison staff work in a house of law. But neither side is above the law. Sadly, many will use that badge, (acting under color of law) to violate your rights. They hope you will not exercise this First Amendment Right to grieve the incident.

So remember to name the right violated and state who violated this right. If you do not know his name then describe that officer—weight, height, color of hair, age and the shift they were working. Name the assignment that staff member was working. Try to describe the person as in detail as possible.

Then state how that person violated your right, or rights. Keep it simple and to the point. Remember this, my fellow convict: do not lie if you seek to go to the court for review. Polygraph examinations are allowed in civil rights violation cases. If you are given a polygraph examination and pass the judge hearing your case will place a lot of weight on this development. If you fail the judge could dismiss your case.

If the staff member refuses to submit to a polygraph test and you pass one, the Judge will see the truth in matters. Most times there is a witness to the incident. Any prisoner who testifies in your case is protected from retaliation or harassment by the prison staff. This is a First Amendment-protected activity found under the U.S. Constitutions Bill of Rights. See the Case Law here developed by the U.S. Seventh Circuit Court of Appeal: *Bridges-vs-Gilbert, 557 F. 3d 541 (7th Cir. 2009)*

Jimmy Bridges filed an affidavit for a prisoner's family. He witnessed the abuse that took place before that prisoner died. The state prison staff reat-liated against him for this help given to the deceased prisoner's family. He filed suit and won. The law is the law. Grievance procedure extends to your witnesses being protected under the First Amendment too. So make sure your witness knows this case so that he can feel free to sign an affidavit and testify. For if that witness is retaliated against, he or she can then bring their own First Amendment activity retaliation case.

You will have 30 days to send the Chief Administrative Officer's response to the ARB in Springfield. Once the Warden signs off on it the 30-day rule starts. If it does not reach Springfield within 30 days they will call a technicality. If the submission is late, they will not respond.

The Prisoner mail box rule comes in to effect here. As long as it is post marked within the 30-days timeline, all will be well. So if you mail it out within 30 days, it is all proper by law.

I always sent the papers out in a large manila envelope and get a receipt from the trust fund officer with the date it was submitted for processing in the institutional mail. Once you place it in the bars, or drop it in a mail box, the date is set—the prison mailbox rule comes into effect.

The address for the Administrative Review Board is:

> Administrative Review Board
> PO Box 19277
> Springfield, IL 62794-9277

REMEMBER, the Administrative Review Board and the Prisoner Review Board are two separate state bodies. They have two separate addresses. The Administrative Review Board deals with issues happeneing in the prison whole you are serving your sentence. The Prisoner Review Board deals with mandatory supervised release (MSR) issues, parole, release sites and MSR violation hearings

> Prisoner Review Board
> 319 East Madison Street
> Suite A
> Springfield, IL 62701

CHAPTER TWO
YOUR BASIC RIGHTS

The Eighth Amendment of our great Constitution guarantees each state prisoner four basic rights.

Our ignorance is often used against us to deny us what we have coming by law. Thus, the need for our forefathers to protect us with the Eight Amendment prohibitions on subjecting prisoners to cruel and unusual punishment. Our forefathers drafted a great Constitution that allowed the public to set the standards of treatment for the American citizen sentenced to prison. One is sent to prison as punishment, but not to be further punished at the hands of sadistic guards and abusive staff.

As the Constitution protects us from abusive treatment, the grievance system was set up to voice these violations. Thus, the Eight Amendment protects us from cruel and unusual punishment. The First Amendment protects us from retaliatory acts for exercising this First Amendment right to complain about the conditions of confinement. Every person sent to a state oe federal facility is guarantee four basic rights under this concept of law.

1. Adequate medical care.
2. A diet to sustain your health.
3. Clothing adequate for your environment.
4. A safe and secure place to serve your sentence.

Now when these rights are violated, the protections under the U.S. Constitution's First Amendment kick in. Every prisoner has the right to complain about his conditions of confinement.

For so many years now I have listened to the same old defeatist talk, which is why I had to write this book. "No, I am not going to file a grievance. If I do that staff will hassle me," a prisoner will say. There is nothing more wrong, and nothing that leads to bigger violations of the law, than to think this way and allow staff to deter this First Amendment Right.

Many of our fellow prisoners, both men and women, have followed the grievance procedure and been punished for it. They rode out the retaliatory storm. Then they went to the federal court and proved up the illegal activity that was going on in the penal system.

They took on the battle and won in order to get these illegal acts exposed, severe penalties imposed on the state employee and compensation won. For these constitutional violations will find the light of day in the federal courts if you exhaust your grievance procedure correctly. So let me break down the two precedent-setting cases in the Seventh Circuit Court of Appeal that directly apply here.These two prisoners had the balls to take on the man and buck the system. They paid the dues for all of us.

The State of Illinois Department of Corrections falls under the U.S. Seventh Circuit Court of Appeal. They hold jurisdiction here. They enforce your Constitutional Rights in the IDOC facilities we all find ourselves living in.

Let us first review the case of, Raul C. Gomez, at Stateville Correctional Center.

Correctional Center prisoner. *Gomez-vs-Randle, 680 F. 3d 859 (7th Cir. 2012)* You will find this case in the *Federal Reporter,* a series of three books located in your law library (*Federal Reporter*, F. 2d and F. 3d).

In May of 2009, Mr. Gomez was a prisoner serving a sentence at the Stateville maximum security prison. This old joint is located in Will County, Illinois, just outside of Joliet—a rough big house to do time in. Statesvill Correctional Center has the last prison round house in America. (A round house is a circular building with a gun tower built in the center. The guard in the tower can see and shoot into any cell.) The East House and West House have five long galleries on each side., five stories straight up. Mr. Gomez was housed there.

On the date of May 16th, 2009, Mr. Gomez was standing outside his cell door waiting to be keyed in. In an instant a fight broke out a few cells away. A guard walking the catwalk fired his shotgun into the men to break up the fight. Mr. Gomez was hit in the arm, a ball entering his bicep muscle. The prison went on lockdown.

After the fight was under control Mr. Gomez reported the injury to the gallery officer. He requested medical care. But none was to come due to the lockdown status. Thus, deliberate indifference to his medical needs started there. This very act of denying medical care violated the Eighth Amendment protections from cruel and unusual punishment.

Mr. Gomez treated his own wound and then filed a grievance seeking medical treatment for the infected arm. Mr. Gomez waited four days until he was taken to the health care unit for treatment. Once there the arm was treated and a paper trail was started in his medical file.

Next an internal affairs investigator (IA) showed up to talk to Mr. Gomez. Hell, every prisoner knows when IA shows up it is normally not a good thing. Thus, the second act of a constitutional violation started to take place. The IA investigator threatened Mr. Gomez with segregation placement and a transfer to the Menard Prison for filing the grievance. Mr. Gomez had enemies housed at Menard. This illegal act of intimidation violated his First Amendment protections. Now we have the Eighth Amendment violation with the lack of medical care and then the IA investigator violated the First Amendment to the U.S. Constitution by threatening Mr. Gomez, hoping he would drop the grievance. Mr. Gomez was placed in segregation and shipped to Menard.

Mr. Gomez exercised his grievance procedure on these issues. He then filed a civil rights 42 U.S.C. § 1983 complaint in the U.S. Northern District. The violations took place at the Stateville Prison. The Northern District Court holds jurisdiction there. The District Court dismissed the case in error. Mr. Gomez appealed the case to the U.S. Seventh Circuit of Appeal. This Court is located in Chicago, Illinois. There his case was re-instated and the work of the District Court went under review. The mistake made was pointed out. Then the real issue of the retaliation for First Amendment activity was addressed by this High Court.

1. Excessive Force, being shot for no reason, was addressed.
2. Deliberate Indifference to his medical needs was addressed.
3. The Retaliation for filing the grievance was addressed.

So now I quote a little of the law here for your review. "C. Retaliation. Finally Gomez asserts a claim of retaliation in violation of his First Amendment right to use the prison grievance system. The district court failed to address this claim entirely in its opinion dismissing Gomez's complaint. Again, we find that Gomez's complaint properly states a claim for relief. [12] [13] To prevail on his First Amendment retaliation claim, Gomez must show that "(1) he engaged in activity protected by the First amendment; (2) he suffered a deprivation that would likely deter First Amendment activity in the future; and (3) the First Amendment activity was at least a motivation factor in the Defendant's decision to take the retaliatory action."

"*Bridges-vs-Gilbert, 557 F.3d 541, 546 (7th Cir. 2009)* (quoting Wood-*Ruff-vs-Mason, 542, F.3d 545, 551 (7th Cir. 2008)*). Gomez easily satisfies all three prongs at the pleading stage. [14] First, Gomez alleges that he used the prison grievance system to address his injury and the lack of treatment he received following his injury. 'A prisoner has a First Amendment right to make grievances about conditions of confinement.' *Watkin-vs-Kasper, 599 F. 3d 791, (7th Cir. 2010).* In addition, Gomez suffered a deprivation when he was transferred from Stateville to Menard where he had known enemies. "[A]n act in retaliation for the exercise of a constitutionally protected right is actionable under Section 1983 even if the act, when taken for different reasons, would have been proper. *Howland-vs-Kilquist, 833 f.2d 639, 644 (7th Cir. 1987).* Moreover, it can be inferred that this punishment would likely deter future First Amendment activity.

Finally, Gomez alleges that the IA investigator, sent to intimidate him by I.D.O.C. Director Randle, threatened Gomez with a transfer to Menard. Even after Gomez indicated that he would no longer pursue his grievance or file a lawsuit if he could stay at Stateville, he was told it was "too late." No other explanation for Gomez's transfer is available at this early stage in *867 the proceedings. Thus, we conclude from Gomez's complaint that his grievance was a motivating factor in the defendant's decision to transfer him to Menard. Because Gomez properly asserted a claim for retaliation, his complaint was prematurely dismissed.. . . For the foregoing reasons, we AFFIRM in part, REVERSE in part, and REMAND this matter to the district court for proceedings consistent with this opinion.

Remember, when filing the grievance , if you don't know the offending officer, try to identify the person to the best of your ability. Then once the case gets past the Exhaustion of State Remedies stage, file a Motion In Discovery to produce the work records and identify the defendant. It is your job to identify the defendant as soon as possible. The Judge will like your moxie here. The Judge will order the State to identify the employee if you file the Discovery Motion identifying the date, shift and job assignment.

Now this case here is a great one for starting your Shepard's list—a Shepard's list is a computer-generated list of cases dealing with the same constitutional question and principle of law. The computer will kick out a list of the same types of cases for review . You can use this to establish precedence in the law. In this case, the Shepard's list contained the First Amendment retaliation claim cases. Mr. Gomez again proved up the law here. No staff in the prison system can harass, confront you, or retaliate against you for filing a proper grievance. Remember, at first his claim was on the Eighth Amendment issue of cruel and unusual punishment, relating to his medical claim after being shot.

Then once the Internal Affairs Investigator threatened him, and had him transferred to Menard, the second claim under the First Amendment was established here. Now there are numerous acts that can lead to a retaliation claim. Perhaps you filed a grievance on the commissary. Now you are treated differently when you shop. You are last to be served. There is problems with your list. You are denied items for no logical reason. Now you have a First Amendment retaliation grievance to be brought.

If you help someone else by being the witness to an incident you are also protected from retaliatory acts. So let us review another strong Seventh Circuit Court of Appeal case. *Bridges-vs-Gilbert, 557 F.3d 541 (7th Cir. 2009) at Key Note* 1.

Jimmy Bridges was a prisoner at the Wisconsin Secure Program Facility. While housed there he witnessed an incident where the prisoner in the cell next to him was assaulted by staff. Then that prisoner passed away. Mr. Bridges supplied that family with an affidavit stating the facts he did witness. The prisoner who died had family that brought a wrongful death claim. With the help of Bridges affidavit the family won in Summary Judgment stage. The case was settled.

The prison staff turned up the heat on Mr. Bridges. They were not happy about the affidavit he had submitted. This was their motivation behind their acts. His mail was delayed beyond reason. One guard would go by and kick the door while he was sleeping. The guard would turn on his light, and slam the chuck hole open and then shut. False tickets followed. But Bridges documented the attacks and filed the grievances.

When Jimmy Bridges brought the suit the State countered that signing an affidavit for someone else is not a protected First Amendment activity like writing a grievance. In this case the Seventh Circuit Court of Appeal cited the law protecting witnesses when they step forward and state what they were a party too. That is why this case is a must-read case. It will teach you the rights that most convicts do not understand or believe that they have. If you read the Gomez and Bridges cases the myth that prison staff can harass you for filing a grievance will be put to rest—for knowledge is key.

In his decision, the Federal Court Judge refers to many other cases he relies on to reach his decision. If you read these Opinions, you may learn many things. You learn the way the Court will interpret the law, the law governing the house you find yourself living in. The U.S. Constitution applies to all prisoners housed in a state facility. These cases apply all across America, in every state.

CHAPTER THREE
FILING A MEDICAL GRIEVANCE

The Medical Grievance in Illinois Department of Corrections is a real monster. As in many other states, the State of Illinois contracted the job out to the Wexford Medical Care Company of Pittsburg, Pennsylvania. They are paid around one-hundred and ten million dollars a year to supply the health care in the Illinois penal system. This is the flaw in the system, the fly in the ointment, because the contractor is allowed to keep all the money they do not spend on supplying health care.

What this creates is a system built to fail. Corporate policy dictates denial of treatment. Deny, deny, deny, and medical employees get a bigger bonus at the end of the year. So one must learn how to protect oneself and get the required treatment required by the law. That means filing the correct grievance to get the process started, using the correct medical and legal terms to be stated on the grievance.

DELIBERATE INDIFFERENCE

The wording of the grievance and complaint must be right. A constitutional claim over denial of adequate medical care requires using the term "deliberate indifference." For example, "Acting with deliberate indifference to my medical needs the following defendants left me in daily pain and suffering." Then you lay out the facts. Dates, times, persons who refused to treat you. You must name each person and give the chronological order of events. You can only seek damages from those defendants actually involved in your request for medical treatment. Remember, the warden (the chief administrative officer) is responsible for making sure the contractors working for him perform their jobs correctly. So write him asking him to make the defendants give you adequate medical care. A letter, or the emergency grievance procedure (which you can indicate on the grievance form) applies here.

Medical malpractice is a term to be used when you file a claim in state court. If ones tries to use this term in a Constitutional Eighth Amendment claim it will be dismissed and referred to the State Court to hear. So when you decide to take action your grievance must be worded to fit the Federal or State court you will be filing in. (Deliberate indifference 8th Amendment claims are for the federal court; medical malpractice is brought in the state court in the prisoner's jurisdiction.) Both courts are there for your use. You must research your claim and decide where to go to seek redress.

THE LAW OF THE LAND

The United States Supreme Court is the big dog in America. What they say is law. What they determine is the law of the land. All States must adhere to the Constitution first and foremost. We fought a Civil War over this fact in the 1800s. The buck stops with their assessment of the law. The "deliberate indifference" standard was set down by the U.S. Supreme Court. It is based on the Eighth Amendment claim protection against cruel and unusual punishment. See *Estelle-vs-Gamble, 97 S, Ct. 285 91976*)

At Key Note 8 the Honorable U.S. Supreme Court Justice wrote it out in his opinion. So I will quote this mighty opinion and then I will break it down into simple terms. Again, everything starts with writing the correct grievance—the grievance must be completed correctly.

Key Note 8, Civil Rights Law key 13.4(5) & Criminal Law Key 1213

"Deliberate indifference to serious medical needs of prisoners constitutes unnecessary and wanton infliction of pain proscribed by the Eighth Amendment whether the indifference is manifested by prison doctors in response to prison needs or by prison guards in intentionally denying or delaying access to medical care or intentionally interfering with treatment once prescribed; regardless of how evidenced, deliberate indifference to prisoner's serious illness or injuries states a cause of action under civil rights statute. U.S.C.A Const. Amend. 8; 42 U.S.C.A. 1983."

The law is the law, and no one is above it. Your grievance must state the statute, (an enactment made by a legislature and expressed in a formal document) and the Constitutional Amendment that was violated, who violated it and how it was violated. Then you must state how you were made to suffer. Let's break this down so the average Joe Convict can understand the law.

BAD TOOTH EXAMPLE

On the date of May 1st, Joe Convict woke with an abscessed tooth. His jaw was swollen. He felt sick. He had a fever, and requested to see a dentist as an emergency. The medical technician at sick call decided it was not an emergency but put prisoner, Joe Convict, on the waiting list. Joe Convict was sent back to his cell without being seen by a dentist.

Two weeks later Joe Convict became very sick. The abscessed tooth had reached critical stage. The infection had entered his blood stream. He was rushed to an outside hospital for emergency dental surgery.

So the deliberate indifference started with the medical technician making a medical call that he was not trained to make. The medical technician is not qualified to determine any treatment or decide on whether you should be seen right away on the tooth issue. So the prisoner must take action to get by this stage of denial. The prisoner should have filed an emergency grievance to the warden. If you are in deep pain and really ill, you may bypass the unqualified screening program (the medical technician's evaluation of the prisoner's medical needs). In situations like this, the prisoner should go straight to the chief administrative officer under your right to file the emergency grievance.

COST OF TREATMENT

With the current sad situation of contracted care, the prisoner is often denied required treatment to save on yearly overhead—to create the bigger, better,bonus at the end of the year. So again you must stand on your rights to adequate medical treatment under the U.S. Constitution—the Bill of Rights at the Eighth Amendment. You may hear the nurse practitioner or the doctor, state that your request will be reviewed at a "collegial hearing." This means nothing but a smoke screen to deny treatment. It means: "Of or characterized by the collective responsibility shared by each of a group of colleagues with minimal supervision from above."

So you have the medical staff at your prison in a meeting to decide whether they will give you the required treatment—not a good situation where yearly overhead determines the person's bonus. So let me give you the example most common in Illinois, the prisoner hernia case. It is a medical fact that only surgery can repair a hernia. To leave a prisoner to suffer daily in pain and discomfort to save on the cost of surgery violates the Eighth Amendment.

In this "collegial hearing" the staff decide whether your required treatment will be scheduled. The prisoner who breaks a finger, leg or arm requires immediate care. The prisoner who dislocates a finger or any joint requires immediate care, for to delay treatment means the bones will not mend properly. If not properly aligned, the joint, the socket, the bone starts to heal abnormally with permanent disfigurement or loss of use. Here you have a claim.

So one must state the set of events in chronological order and name the people involved in the denial of medical care.

Here is an unpublished case that is a must read, the Danville Correctional Center case of *Myrick-vs-Anglin, 496 Fed. Appx. 670 (7th Cir. 20120).* (Not all cases heard in the federal courts are placed in the federal books, so are not published in the *Federal Reporter*. Unpublished orders are made by the trial judge, often requested by the attorney general's office.) This case deals with several medical issues where the prisoner was denied care. A hernia was one of the issues. The contractor (Wexford Medical) will leave you suffering daily with a hernia simply because they do not want to pay for the surgery. This case dealt with that fact. The prisoner was left to suffer daily as he tried to move his bowels, owrk out and generally live. See these cases also.

Gonzales-vs-Fienerman, 663 F. 3d 311 (7th Cir. 2011)

Taylor-vs-Plousis, 101 F.Supp. 2d 255 (D.N.J. 2000)

All these cases deal with denial of adequate medical care to save on cost. Read them before you start writing your grievance. For they are a guideline in drafting the correct grievance.

MEDICAL DIET CASE LAW

To obtain a medical diet, you must to to the health care unit and establish your condition or disease. The order for a specail diet will be placed in your master file and medical files.

Once you have a medical diet established at one prison and you get shipped to another facility, the medical staff cannot cancel your diet, nor can they deny your prior treatment. When you require a medical diet and the prison dietary manager or health care director denies your diet, these cases will help you draft the correct grievance in this situation.

Sellers-vs-Henman, 41 F.3d 1100, 1102 (7th Cir. 1994)

Morales Feliciano-vs-Calderon Sierra, 300 F. Supp. 2d 341 (D.P.R. 2004)

Woulard-vs-Food Services, 294 F. Supp. 2d 596, 604 (D. Del 2003)

Mandala-vs-Couglin, 920 F. Supp. 342, 355 (E.D.N.Y. 1996)

MENTAL HEALTH CASE LAW

The State is required to supply mental health care. No longer can segregation be used as a means to house and deal with the mentally ill prisoner. See the recent case of *Rasho-vs-Walker, U.S. CD Peoria Division, No. 1:07-cv-1298-MMM-JAG*, which set new guidelines on treatment of the mentally ill. SMI (severely mentally ill) is now a recognized condition where the prisoner must be allowed to stay in population and be given the same routine and privileges. That prisoner is now housed in a single cell with a magnetic strip above the door marked SMI.

Regarding treatment of the SMI, change has finally come to the prisons, at least in the state of Illinois. These cases will help anyone draft the appropriate grievance and get the correct care for any prisoner who is severlyt mentally ill.

Gates-vs-Cook, 376 F.3d 323, 343 (5th Cir. 2004)

Dolihite-vs-Maughon By and Through Videon, 74 F .3d 1027, 1042 (11th Cr. 1996)

Joseph-vs-Brierton, 739 F.2d 1244, 1246 (7th Cir. 1984)

SEX OFFENDER PROGRAMS

Many sex offender cases are mandated treatment by the judge passing sentence on that case. Therefore, for many to get good time credits, and mandatory supervised release (meaning that supervision is required after the sentence is served), they must complete sex therapy while in the IDOC. Therefore, it is a required treatment that must be provided to the prisoner. See this case law here:

Sundby-vs-Fielder, 827 F.Supp. 580, 583 (W.D. Wis. 1993)

Patterson-vs-Webster, 760 F.Supp. 150, 153-54 (E.D.MO 1991)

McKune-vs-Lile, 536 U.S. 24, 35-36, 122 S.Ct. 2017 (2002)

Callender-vs-Sioux City Residential Treatment Facility, 88 F.3d 666, 668 (8th Cir. 1996)

DENTAL CARE CASE LAW

In the IDOC we have a long waiting line to see the dentist. But dental hygiene and tooth repair cannot be denied to the prisoner. Emergency treatment for abscessed teeth is a must since an untreated abscessed tooth can cause mental illness and even death. Once the poison from the abscess reaches your blood stream you are in real danger. So file the correct emergency grievance if you find yourself in this situation.

Board-vs-Farnham, 394 F.3d 469, 481-82 (7th Cir. 2005)

Wynn-vs-Southward, 251 F.3d 588, 593 (7th Cir. 2001)

Matzker-vs-Herr, 748 F.2d 1142, 1147-48 (7th Cir. 1984)

All these cases requiring a medical care claim have prior case law behind it. Run a Shepard's list on the Eight Amendment Deliberate Indifference search stating your particular medical need. Then use the case law in preparing your grievance. Every prisoner has the right under the U.S. Constitution to adequate medical care.

I must recommend a book to every prisoner who wants to pursue a claim to the federal court system. Get a copy of the P*risoner's Self-Help Litigation Manual, Fourth Edition*. It is written by John Boston and Daniel E. Manville. This book will guide you through each step of the proceedings. You can order it through the *Prison Legal News Magazine*. A must for all *pro se* litigators behind these walls and fences in any state.

I have a favorite saying, "It ain't no fun when the rabbit has the gun." Well, this book will give you the knowledge and power to litigate with the best that any state attorney general's office has to offer. Knowledge is power. This book is that knowledge in hand.

CHAPTER FOUR

FILING A GRIEVANCE FOR ADEQUATE CLOTHING

Under the Eight Amendment to the U.S. Constitution each prisoner is given protection from cruel and unusual punishment. To deny a prisoner adequate clothing for the environment he or she is subjected to states (or required) a claim. The court has established the fact that the prisoner must be given two sets of clothing, one to wear while one is being washed. Furthermore, the penal facility is required by law to supply laundry service at a minimum of once a week. Clothing walks hands-in-hand with society's hygiene requirements. The concept of civilized society that applies to prison conditions.

If you are not given the adequate clothing you feel you need, then you must name the person responsible for denying it. The gallery officer is not the culprit here. He only sends the request to the clothing house supervisor. If you are going to challenge the current policy in place the clothing house supervisor is the one to name in your grievance. You must state all interaction with him or her and the policy being applied toward you. See this case: *Knop-vs-Johnson, 667 F. Supp. 467, 475-77 (W.D. Mich. 1987)*

This was a case where the Michigan convicts complained the clothing was not warm enough to face their severe winter conditions. They won the issue. Adequate jackets, hats, gloves and heavy boots and socks were then issued.

In the later rulings by the Seventh Circuit Court of Appeal harsher standards were applied toward the prisoner. The outcome was not good. See this case here. *Mays-vs-Springborn, 573 F.3d 643, 648-49 (7th Cir. 2009)* holding that, "the court rejects the claim of inadequate clothing for the winter as no more than the usual discomfort of winter."

So with the adequate clothing issue, we are seeing a constant change in how the law is and will be applied. This is one where the prisoner must research the current standard and work with it. The prisoner should create a Shepard's list citing this case forward to present day. If a prisoner is required to live on state pay each month, then he has a better chance of prevailing, for the U.S. Constitution states the legal obligation of protecting the impoverished prisoner from cruel and unusual punishment.

But on the flip side, if the prisoner has a monthly balance of fifty dollars or higher, the court will not hesitate to state that you can buy your own extra clothing. So it is a two-sided sword here. Your Constitution protects the poor, but will not hesitate to dismiss this claim if you have money to buy extra clothing to wear in the winter months. The Court will require a six-month print-out from your trust fund account to determine this question.

LAUNDRY SERVICE

All prisoners are entitled to clean clothing, to have the opportunity to get it cleaned or the ability to clean it themselves. The departments of correction are required by law to provide weekly laundry service as well as an adequate change of clothing to last a week—a clean set to wear while the dirty ones are being washed. Here are a few cases to get a better understanding of your rights here.

Divers-vs-Dep't of Corrections, 921 F.2d 191, 194 (8th Cir. 1990)

Holding that "adequate laundry service required."

Howard-vs-Adkinson, 887 f.2d 134, 137 (8th Cir. 1989)

Holding that "the lack of clean clothing or a way to launder clothing for an extended period of time could be unconstitutional."

Landfair-vs-Sheahan, 878 F. Supp. 1106, 1112 (N.D. Ill. 1995)

Here is an interesting set of circumstances that came into play at the Menard Maximum Security Section, November and December of 2015. The laundry machines broke down. They were removed from service and sent out of the facility for repair.

1. Here the prison has a legitimate excuse for not washing his clothes every week.

2. But they must allow the prisoner a means and way to clean his or her own clothes. Therefore laundry soap must be supplied, or an opportunity to go to commissary to buy it. The staff must relax the rules on hanging up line to dry your clothing on. A compromise must be allowed here. Otherwise you have a grievance with merit here.

See Wilson-vs-Cook County Bd. of Commissioners, 878 F. Supp. 1163, 1169 (N.D. Ill. 1995) holding that; "allegations of the uniforms had not been changed in a month, among other sanitation issues, stated an Eighth Amendment Claim."

Reese-vs-Gragg, 650 F. Supp. 1297, 1305 (D.Kan. 1986)

Toussaint-vs-Rushen, 553 F. Supp. 1365, 1371, 1379, 1385 (N.D. Cal. 1983)

Holding that lack of regular laundry service is unconstitutional:

Martino-vs-Carey, 563 F. Supp. 984, 1000 (D.Or. 1983)

"Under certain circumstances the prisoner may be required to wash his clothes in his cell. Under these certain circumstances the state must relax rules and work with the prisoners until the problem with institutional laundry service is resolved.

Green-vs-Farrell, 801 F.2d 765, 771 (5th Cir. 1986)

Shelby County Jail Inmates-vs-Westlake, 798 F.2d 1085, 1091 (7th Cir. 1986)

Benjamin-vs-Fraser, 161 F. Supp. 2d at 178-79

If your clothes do not fit, are torn, or they are coming apart, you can get them repaired by contacting the clothing room supervisor. Remember to keep a copy of all written requests. Clothing is a basic human requirement you have coming by law. Remember the process:

1. Counselor
2. Grievance Officer
3. Administrative Review Board

Keep copies of all filings!

CHAPTER FIVE
GRIEVANCES REGARDING DIET

Currently this is a very tricky grievance. The Eighth Amendment to the U.S. Constitution requires the state penal system to supply the prisoner with a diet to sustain his health. It is truly illegal to serve a detrimental diet for the sole reason of saving money on the dietary budget. This is the evil monster we were saddled with in the Illinois Department of Corrections.

Governor Blagojevich got into bed with the Archer Daniel Midland Company in 2003 and instituted a prison diet that was 70 percent soy—fake soy "meat," soy cheese, even soy in the baking mixes. We have been dealing with this fact every since. (This diet was only for the men; the women stopped menstruating on this diet and after protests, it was discontinued.)

We got the soy sludge diet in place of meat because state funds started to dry up. The State of Illinois was spending more then they were taking in. The prison dietary budget was the first item to be placed on the state comptroller's chopping block.

Many men got sick. Unlike the women prisoners, the men did not know how to write up the effects they were suffering from. They could not tie the soy to their illness. They suffered from digestive problems and thyroid disorders. The high estrogen levels in soy affected the male testosterone levels and hence heart rate and muscle function. Some men grew breasts. They called the soy diet "chemical castration."

A man needed to be a doctor or biochemist to figure out that medical nightmare. I was lucky to have several ladies on the outside willing to enlighten me on the dangers of soy. In August of 2007 I filed a case in the U.S. Central District Court in Springfield, Illinois, the first case on soy in the prisoner diet. By December of 2008 the state medical contractor, Wexford, gave in. They issued the blood test and found that I had developed Hashimoto's thyroiditis disease. In December of 2008 I was issued the first no-soy medical diet by Dr. Shah.

I had trouble getting the no-soy diet when I was transferred to another prison, but I was always able to get it re-instated once I challenged the medical issue. For once you have a thyroid disorder it is medical deliberate indifference to continue to make the prisoner survive off a soy-based diet—it's like telling a lung cancer patient to smoke two packs of cigarettes a day. Soy consumption exacerbates the disease, causing daily pain and suffering from the hypothyroidism symptoms—in violation of the Eight Amendment prohibitions on cruel and unusual punishment. Can you dig it?

Unfortunately, after my last transfer, they took away my no-soy diet so I had to go to court again. See *Harris, et al.,-vs-Brown, et al., 3:07-cv-03225-HAB-BGC.* I did not win that round but then something happened that was a win for all the prisoners. On January 1, 2019, the IDOC discontinued the soy diet and started serving meat again. My guess is that they did not want the liability of so many prisoners sick with thyroid and other diseases.

The following case law further expands on your right to a healthy diet in prison.

"Obligation of state to provide inmate with healthy habilitative environment includes obligation to provide nutritionally adequate food that is prepared and served under conditions which do not present immediate danger to health and well-being of inmates who consume it. U.S.C.A. Const. Amend. 8

Ramos-vs-Lamm, 639 f.2d 559 (10th Cir. 1980) at Key Note 8;
310 Prisons; 310 II Prisoners and Inmates;
310 II (B) Care, Custody, Confinement, and Control;
310k57 k. Food and Drink (formerly 310k17, 310k17)

"A lack of financing is not a defense to a failure to satisfy minimum constitutional standards in prisons."

Duran-vs-Anaya, 642 F. Supp. 510 (D.New Mex. 1986) at Key Note

So let's break these down. The State is required to serve you a meal that will sustain your health, not one that makes you sick each day. The idea they can do this to save money on their state dietary budget is rebutted in the *Duran-vs-Anaya* case. So you have two cases here that state the law. The diet served must sustain your health. The law is the law here. The budget crisis and kick-back deals are not a defense to this Constitutional requirement under the 8th Amendment prohibitions of cruel and unusual punishment. For it is cruel and unusual punishment to be fed a meal each day that makes the prisoners sick.

If you feel your diet is not keeping your healthy, you must state on your grievance the symptoms you suffer from. Take a look at the symptoms of hypothyroidism and low testosterone levels. That the diet is inadequate due to budget cuts might fly if you can show you are not getting the required calories and nutrients daily.

Then we all have the issue of the pilfering of the prion dietary budget to buy special meals for the prison staff. This misapplication of dietary budget funds is illegal. This misapplication of funds to supply staff with a soy-free meal each day, while the prisoners must eat soy, violates the state dietary statutes concerning free meals for the staff. The law states the officer working may have a choice of the two meals fed to the prisoner population. The law is clear here that the officer is to eat the same meal served to the prisoner on the lunch and supper tray, or the supper and breakfast tray. No special diet is to be prepared daily simply because the staff do not want to consume the soy-based diet that the prisoner has to eat. This is an issue that should be raised by every prisoner in his or her grievance. The law is the law, and neither side is above it. Unfortunately, the staff has been stealing these dietary funds and serving this illegal meal for so long they believe they have it coming by law.

SPECIAL DIETS

Prison officials, both medical and dietary directors, are required by law and constitutionally obligated to supply the special religious diets as well as medical diets. We covered the medical diet issue in chapter three. Now we address the religious one. We will address the interpretation of this matter as set by the U.S. Supreme Court—we can't do any better then the rules of the big dog in this land. The case law I provide here is essential in filing this grievance. Getting the religious diet becomes harder each year due to budget cuts. The prison diet budget for the prisoner population is always where they start cutting expenses—a sad state of affairs that makes it so one must stand on the law to enforce his or her rights to this diet sought.

Under the First Amendment to the U.S. Constitution these rights are clearly developed. The First Amendment also protects the right of the "establishment of religion," which means that the government must support and provide sponsorship of religion. The Religious Freedom Restoration Act, (RFFA), and the Religious Land Use and Institutionalized Act, (RLUIPA), set the law here.

These acts give you the law and statutes needed to write a winning grievance to win your religious diet. They are federal law statutes that can be found in your prison law library.

42 U.S.C. § 2000cc-5(7)(A) and 42 U.S.C. § will be the right statutes for this issue. The Court stated, "This Act shall be construed in favor of a broad protection of religious exercise, to the maximum extent permitted by the terms of this Act and the Constitution." See 42 U.S.C. § 2000bb-2(4). It therefore seems to be a logical legal argument to conclude that anything that courts have found to be protected by the free exercise clause is also protected by the RLUIPA and RFRA.

So if your religion requires a certain diet then you have the right to this diet, even in prison. Your grievance should start with the chaplain and dietary manager of your prison, and then you must exhaust all three steps before you can seek a federal court order to supply the diet. Sadly, in Illinois, they may force you to this extreme.

The Courts have ruled that a prisoner has a right to a diet consistent with his or her religious scruples and doctrine. But the actual outcome of prison religious diets cases has been a two-sided sword. Under the Turner Standard delivered many courts have rules the prison must supply the diet. See U.S. Supreme Court case of *Turner-vs-Safely, 107 S.Ct. 2254 (1987)* to understand the principle of the law applied here. The courts have ruled that the special diets should not place an extreme burden on the prison staff.

Dehart-vs-Horn, 390 F.3d 262, 269-70 (3rd Cir. 2004)

Holding that the individualized preparation of the Mahayuana Buddist diet requiring avoidance of pungent vegetables was too much of a burden for the prison staff.

Williams-vs-Morton, 343 F 3d 212, 218 (3rd Cir 2002)

Kahey-vs-Jones, 836 F 2d. 948, 949-50 (5th Cir. 1988)

Other courts have ruled that prisoner complaints raise a valid First Amendment claim. But the court has ruled against the prisoner in cases where the denial was reasonably related to budget and administrative concerns, for example a case where the cost and requirement allowing the individual prisoner to prepare his own meal was denied. So remember to make sure your diet is served in the prison, for if one can get it, all can get it. There is no discriminatory policy allowed.

All holding the right to diet clearly established in these cases.

Ford-vs-McGinnis, 352 F.3d 582, 597 (2nd Cir. 2003)

Beerheide-vs-Suthers, 286 F.3d 1179, 1185 (10th Cir. 2002)

Jackson-vs-Mann, 196 F.3d 316, 321 (2nd Cir. 1999)

PORK ISSUE

These are Muslim cases where prison officials had to show the court why they refused to stop serving pork to Muslims in segregation.

Hunafa-vs-Murphy, 907 F.2d 46,47 (7th Cir. 1990)

Omar-vs-Casterline, 288 F.Supp. 775, 781-82 (W.D. La 2003)

RAMADAN DIET

McEachin-vs-McGinnis, 357 F.3d 197, 203-05 (2003)

Conyers-vs-Abitz, 416 F.3d 580, 585-86 (7th Cir. 2005)

Remember to use the Shapard's ist to generate the latest case law applied here.

Kogers-vs-Bryan, 523 F.3d 789, 800-02 (7th Cir. 2008)

One must remember this, "The State is required to supply a diet to sustain the prisoner's health" not one that is detrimental to the prisoner's health and well-being in order to save money on the dietary budget.

ONCE THE DIET IS ISSUED

Many times the Illinois prisoner will be transferred to another facility. Whether it is a temporary one, as in a court writ status transfer, or a permanent transfer, the prisoner retains the right to that diet. See the prior case law cited above.

If you have a diet like the kosher diet, you must check with the chaplain to get a list of the items on commissary that are not kosher. For if you buy no-kosher items in the commissary, your diet can be terminated. So you must protect your rights here.

CHAPTER 6

MEDICAL COST & DELIBERATE INDIFFERENCE

The Illinois prison system has a "Catch 22" situation many prisoners will find themselves subjected to. The current medical contractor in Illinois is the Wexford Health Sources, Inc.

Wexford Health Sources, Inc.
501 Holiday Drive
Foster Plaza Four
Pittsburg, PA 15220

The system in place is created to fail the prisoner. The IDOC gives Wexford a set amount of money each year to supply health care to the prisoner population in Illinois. Then it lets the contractor keep all the money they do not spend on health care each year. Thus, the Wexford bonus policy was born. Deny, deny, deny treatment is the policy to curb overhead and give a bigger bonus at the end of the year to each employee.

So now you understand why your health care is denied and why the prisoner is told he must pay the five-dollar co-pay three times before being seen by a doctor. These are money-generating policies in place that violate the law, and your right to adequate medical care. I did not write the law, nor do I agree with it. The co-pay is a real problem, but it is a problem we face. So let us address the co-pay statute first.

Public Act # 91-0912 at 730 ILCS 5/3-6-2 Section (£). Under this statute the State of Illinois 91st General Assembly created the public act that allowed the prisoner to be charged a co-pay. So read and review it. Review all the updates too. It was first passed with a two-dollar co-pay in place. That has been amended and raised to a five-dollar fee.

Sadly most Illinois prisoners do not read the law. So they do not understand the rules of the game afoot. So here are some comments for your review. For the game is only fair when both parties know the rules of the playing field.

Any prisoner surviving on the ten dollar a month state pay should never be subjected to a medical co-pay charge. In addition, the prisoner must maintain a balance of twenty dollars or more for thirty days before the request for medical care, a balance of twenty dollars or more for thirty days after the voucher is submitted for the co-pay to be deducted from his or her account. Indigent status forbids this charge.

Here is the law verbatim: "(f) In the event that the person requires medical care and treatment at a place other than the institution or facility, the person may be removed therefrom under conditions prescribed by the Department. The Department shall require the committed person receiving medical or dental services on a non-emergency basis to pay a $2 co-payment to the Department for each visit for medical or dental services at a place other than the institution or facility. The amount of each co-payment shall be deducted from the committed person's individual account. A committed person who has a chronic illness, as defined by Department rules and regulations, shall be exempt from the $2 co-payment for treatment of the chronic illness. A committed person shall not be subject to a $2 co-payment for follow-up visits, ordered by a physician, who is employed by, or contracts with, the Department. A committed person who is indigent is exempt from the $2 co-payment and is entitled to receive medical or dental services on the same basis as a committed person who is financially able to afford the co-payment.""

So here we have two things to understand. First, if you have a balance of over twenty-dollars a month in your account you will be charged. But you can only be charged one time. Then you must be treated by a medical technician or seen by the doctor. Any facility trying to charge you more than once for the same medical issue is in violation of the Public Act statute.

Second, the indigent prisoner surviving off the ten-dollar-a-month state pay stipend cannot be charged for medical care. So if you are charged, file the grievance and stop this illegal practice.

DELIBERATE INDIFFERENCE DUE TO COST

I will use the ugly issue of hernia surgery to describe the situation in the Illinois prisons. When any medical treatment such as surgery, dental care beyond the facility's ability, or emergency situations that arise, like a heart attack, or pacemaker placement, the Wexford Staff will hold a "collegial conference" to discuss and approve or deny the required health care. This is a hearing done by the Wexford medical staff or administrator with the doctor, which is actually an "in-house" discussion on cost verses overhead.

Many times the surgery or required care is denied due to cost. This to curb, or cut, the yearly overhead. This is an illegal act that leaves the prisoner in daily pain and suffering. Only the prisoner and his family care about his pain. So they must step up and start with the grievance. Family calls to the director and governor are always a good way to bring attention to your plight for adequate medical care. For example, the only correct treatment for a hernia is surgery. But the Wexford staff will deny this, leaving the person in daily misery. This violates the law established under the 8th Amendment to the U.S. Constitution. Got yhe prohibitions on cruel and unusual punishment.

I will use the case of *Gonzalez-vs-Feinerman, 663 F.3d 311 (7th Cir. 2011)* as an excellent working format. It is an Illinois Department of Corrections case at the Menard Maximum Security Prison, a great case to research and get an enchanting view of how that law is applied. Mr. Gonzalez brought civil action after he was repeatedly denied surgery at the Menard prison. A prisoner cannot bring a civil rights complaint simply because he does not agree with the treatment prescribed. One must prove that the standard of treatment is below the normal actions of a competent doctor and that the prisoner is left in daily pain and suffering. Then one must complete all three stages of the grievance procedure. A prisoner must attach these copies to the 42 U.S.C.A. § 1983 Civil Petition when it is filed.

In the case of Mr. Gonzalez, he filed a suit claiming the two Wexford doctors and the warden did not provide adequate medical care for his hernia. The medical standard for a hernia is surgery. Be sure to read and study Key Note One, Prison Key Law 192 & Sentencing and Punishment Key Law 1546. Key Note Two sets down the standard of law, the legal liability, which you must be able to prove up. By intentionally disregarding a prisoner's serious medical condition due to cost violates the law. Thus, the doctor and warden are liable. As the warden is the chief administrative officer, it is his job to ensure the medical contractor does his required job correctly. The surgery was given and the prisoner was awarded damages for pain and suffering.

So if you are not getting the required treatment, draft a letter to the warden asking him to take a look at the situation. He now has first-hand knowledge of your situation, a point one must prove up in the process of seeking correct care. In the *Appendix Book to the Federal Reporter Appendix Book* (found in the law library) there is another very interesting Illinois Department of Corrections case. This one was at the Danville Correctional Center (*Myrick-vs-Anglin, 496 fed. Appx. 670 (7th Cir. 2012)*, which also involved a hernia case. Here the prisoner raises other claims too. This is good case law, but an unpublished case the State does not want you to know about.

Plaintiff Myrick was left in daily pain and suffering like Mr. Gonzalez. His condition did get worse as time passed by. Look it up and apply it to your medical deliberate indifference grievance. For the law cited adds great weight to any grievance. The prisoner was given the surgery he needed and damages for pain and suffering. Here are others.

Taylor-vs-Plousis, 101 F.Supp. 2d 255 (D.N.J. 2000)

Starbeck-vs-Linn County Jail, 871 S. Supp. 1129, 1145-46 (N.D. Iowa 1994)

Jackson-vs-Fauver, 334 F. Supp. 2d 697 (D.N.J. 2004) at Key note 3.

If you break a bone and do not get it set immediately it can and will set up and be a problem for life. So you need to stand on correct treatment going in the door. Understand that any medical treatment that requires outside care is going to be a battle. Any situation that leaves you in daily pain and suffering to stay cost states a claim under the Eight Amendment to the U.S. Constitution, the cruel-and-unusual-punishment standard. A grievance on the doctor and warden is required, with an emergency grievance to the warden first. Then follow the correct steps while seeking the recommended medical care.

CHAPTER 7
A SAFE & SECURE ENVIRONMENT TO SERVE YOUR SENTENCE

There are four constitutional rights that come under the Eight Amendment to the U.S. Constitution.

Adequate Medical Care

Adequate Clothing for Your Environment

A Diet To Sustain the Prisoner's Health

The Right to a Safe and Secure Environment to Serve Your Sentence

We now deal with the last of these constitutional rights, the one most violated in the penal system. You have the right to be in a safe cell where you do not have to fight your celly, where you can serve your sentence in peace, a place where you are not subjected to mental, physical or sexual abuse, or worried about your safety on a daily basis.

Here again, we must prove up the deliberate indifference standard to win a grievance and claim. I was housed in the East Cell House at the Menard Maximum Facility in October of 2015, in cell 5-07. On October 7, 2015, at the day shift lunch meal, two men went to fighting in the east cell house dining room. These men were on the bottom gallery, but we all went on lockdown for it.

On October 13, 2015, the East House came off lockdown at lunch time. Around 8:05 a.m., a few minutes after eight in the morning the two guys in cell 3-12 went to fighting. The guy in the cell had a history of assaulting, intimidating and generally stealing from and harassing his cellies. But this morning the victim was not going to be a victim anymore. He took the bully's back and tore both his eyes from their sockets and tossed them on the floor. This is nothing new in the world of maximum security housing. but it should not be so.

Any prisoner who has a history of intimidating, stealing from and assaulting his cellmates should not be double-celled with anyone. Here is where the deliberate indifference standard is proven up. The warden and his staff are responsible. They are required by law to provide a safe living environment for each and every prisoner, regardless of that prisoner's conviction or crime. The prisoner who fought back had developed a long paper trail on the Menard warden. He had requested a cell change numerous times. The Warden was well aware of the aggressive cell mate's past history with cellmates. But the Warden told him, "This is not the Hilton, deal with it." So he did.

On the morning of October 13th, 2015, the little guy had enough. When attacked he defended himself. He blinded the bully. But this never should have reached the point of boiling over. Sadly, the staff did not want to deal with it. They wanted to cram as many bodies in to the cells as possible. Forget the prisoner's rights here. So the bully was dealt poetic justice. He is blind for life. No longer will he prey on his cellmates.

Illinois is notorious for letting this type of thing go down. One reason is they need to generate these types of incidents to keep the segregation cells full. (Segregation cells are punishment cells where all privileges, programs, electronics, property and commissary is restricted and denied.) As a prisoner have you ever wondered why they place antagonistic cellies together? It is to create incidents to keep men in the segregation cells. This is why they started housing blacks and whites together. One prison, Pontiac had too many empty cells. The policy was to move prisoners from population into segregation. This is illegal, and if you find yourself in this situation you need to create a paper trail to cover your backside. So I give the Illinois Department of Corrections case to use as a study guide if you find yourself being placed in this situation by staff. See *Lee-vs-Shepler, U.S.D.C. (C.D. Ill. 2014) Case # 4:11-cv-04064-SLD.*

In this case the prisoner, Lincoln Lee, was housed at the Illinois River Correctional Center The prison was overcrowded. Placement did not want to deal with Lee's request for a cell change. They did not want to investigate or confirm his allegations that his cellmate was threatening him with physical harm. With deliberate indifference to his need for a safe cell to do his time, the staff forced him back into that cell. They gave him the same old bullshit story: "You can refuse housing and go to segregation if you are scared." Thus, the first stage of the deliberate indifference standard was met here.

No prisoner should be forced to subject himself, or herself, to segregation and a disciplinary report for fear of their life and well-being. If the staff refuses to correct the situation, make sure you get their names. Place the date, time, and area having to do with your request for a cell change. Keep these records. There is tall law on this, but it must be stated in your grievance to set the chronological sets of events. The United States Supreme Court set "Precedence" in this legal standard.

Precedence: 1. A Court decision on a question of law that is binding authority on lower courts in the same court system for cases in which those courts must decide a similar question of law involving similar facts.

The U.S. Supreme Court is the law of the land. This issue was addressed by them in *Farmer-vs-Brennan, 511 U.S. 825 (1994)*

Lincoln Lee exhausted his state remedies here. He used this case and went to the federal court seeking redress on the assault he endured while the guards turned a blind eye to his requrest for help, letting his celly assault him, deliberately indifferent to his safety needs. He got paid for the assault he suffered at the hands of his celly.

It was a similar situation with a prisoner named Farmer in the case of *Farmer vs Brennen*. Farmer was a transsexual placed out into the population to be raped and beaten by the prisoners housed in that maximum security prison. The guards turned a blind eye to his need for protection. He got damagesfor the abuse he suffered as well. In fact, his case set the legal standard. Study this case to understand the way the law is interpreted. Then use it to write the correct grievance naming the people who have denied your request for a safe cell while serving your sentence. Name the guard, liuetenant, major, counselor and warden. Keep copies of all letters and the grievance. Record the chronological set of events related to each staff member, for they will become defendants.

Also, when the prison staff knows that a prisoner is mentally ill and cannot be in a cell with another prisoner without problems, they are obligated by law to remove that man or woman from the general population and protect the general population subjection to this type of housing. See the Severely Mentally Ill lawsuit in Illinois: *Rasho-vs-Walker, U.S.D.C. CD Ill. Case # 1:07-cv-01298-MMM.*

It has been common practice to target the "jailhouse lawyer," the inmate who helps other prisoners write their grievances—or any prisoner who stands up for every right they have coming by law. The prison administration will place someone who is severely mentally ill in the cell to target and harass the jailhouse lawyer. This is an illegal act, which must first be addressed through the grievance process. The problem prisoner should not be used by the staff to deter your First Amendment activity in writing a grievance.

So here are some great cases on the prisoner being assaulted by another prisoner and the deliberate indifference of staff to a safe and secure cell to do your time. The prisons can only get away with these practices if we let them.

Babcock-vs-White, 102 F.3d 267,273-74 (7th Cir. 1996)

Jensen-vs-Clarke, 94 F.3d 1191, 1200-01 (8th Cir. 1996)

Cantu-vs-Jones, 293, F. 3d 839, 843-44 (5th Cir. 2002)

Newman-vs-Holmes, 122 F.3d 650, 651 (8th Cir. 1997)

Wright-vs-Jones, 907 F.2d 848, 850, 852 (8th Cir. 1990)

Hutchison-vs-McCabe, 168 F. Supp. 2d 101, 102-04 (S.D.N.Y. 2001)

Noting award of 4392,000.00 for permanent injury that limited plaintiff's future ability to work.

Miller-vs-Shelby County, 93 F. Supp. 2d 892, 902 (W.D. Tenn. 2000)

Awarding $40,000 for impairment of the right shoulder, a scalp puncture wound, and frozen shoulder, headache and blurred vision.

There is quite a bit of law on this issue, for it is a common problem. The prison staff do not want to address the problem. They are too lazy or inept to understand the law. Or they simply do not care and abuse their authority acting under "the color of law," that is, the correctional officer using his badge to violate the law. But we live in a house of law, and they work in house of law—and neither side is above the law. So use the grievance procedure. Remember, a prisoner must always show, *in writing*, that he contacted staff requesting a safe cell and then that the staff refused to act.

The prison staff must protect the prisoner from sexual abuse. Sexual assault by prisoner or staff is forbidden under the PREA act. It can be reported over the phone or a grievance to the warden. This is an emergency grievance that can be sealed and dropped in Institutional mail at your facility. Here is case law on sexual assault:

Lewis-vs-Richards, 107 F.3d 549, 554 (7th Cir. 1997.

Holding: "Exercising poor judgment…falls short of meeting the standard of consciously disregarding a known risk to the prisoner's safety."

Glenn-vs-Bernt, 289 F. Supp. 2d 1120, 1125 (N.D. Cal. 2003)

Holding: "Officer who let black and white prisoners out of their segregation cells during time of racial unrest, but stated it was an accident, was found to be negligent and not deliberately indifferent as required by the Federal Act and Statute."

Negligence in permitting as assault may constitute a tort claim under state law, that is a case where injury resulted from a breach of a legal duty. Tort claims under state court jurisdiction fall under the negligence standard, meaning it was not deliberately done, but it was an act of not doing one's job correctly. That there was no malice of forethought. To understand this concept of the law see:

Goka-vs-Bobbitt, 862 F.2d 646, 651 (7th Cir. 1988)

To better understand the principle of law here. "A constitutional violation is where the defendants know of the danger or where the threat of violence is so substantial that their being told and having knowledge could be inferred. If defendants fail to embrace a policy that takes reasonable steps to prevent the fight or assault they violate the U.S. Constitution under the Eight Amendment."

Clem-vs-Lomeli, 566 F.3d 1177, 1181-82 (9th Cir. 2009) Holding

The jury should have been instructed in the assault case, that defendant's failure to protect, as well as acting, could support a finding of 8th Amendment Deliberate Indifference Claim.

Also see:

Taylor-vs-Michigan Department of Corrections, 69 F. 3d 76, 84 (6th Cir. 1995)

Holding: It was obvious that placing a small, very vulnerable prisoner, in an open, unstructured camp where sexual assault was rampant stated a claim.

Velez-vs-Johnson, 395 F.3d 732, 736 (7th Cir. 2005)

Holding:"Where the prisoner repeatedly pressed the emergency button in the cell, and told the officer he was having a major problem with his celly, the officer's defense that he did not know the celly was holding a jailhouse razor to the prisoner's neck, or that the prisoner would be raped, did not show the officer lacked first hand knowledge that he needed to act on the risk at hand here."

So when you tell the guard, counselor or warden that you are having a serious problem with housing, they are obligated by law to place you in a safe cell to serve your sentence free from assault. If they fail to move you, or act to defuse the situation, or try to force you to refuse housing, you have started your chronological order of events with the grievance. Keep a copy of everything you write. Simply sit down and make two copies. Mail one, and keep the other in your records.

Do not let the lazy or inept actions of staff cost you your life in a jailhouse murder beef. Under the 1996 Prison Litigation Reform Act, the prisoner lost the ability to claim and collect on *mental* anguish and suffering—you must show *physical* pain and suffering. Once it is reported that an assault took place you have a claim and case. See *Farmer-vs-Brennan, 511 U.S. 825 (1994)*

Yes, it is an ugly, very stressful life, to live in a cell with another prisoner you cannot get along with. Use your rights and stop this before it escalates into a read bad situation.

CHAPTER 8
SHELTER

The prisoner has the right to adequate shelter. The correct cell size for two people to live in is set a sixty square feet of living space. The prisoner has a right to adequate lighting and heating, hot and cold running water in the cell and a place to shower. There is constitutional law on all these issues. If a prisoner does not have these basic amenities, it violates his right to be free from cruel and unusual punishment under the Eight Amendment to the U.S. Constitution.

If you are placed in a segregation cell with no electrical outlet and hence no fan, then in the summer months you have claim once the temperature reaches over 90 degrees for three straight days.

Gates-vs-Cook, 376 f.3d 323, 339-40 (5th Cir. 2004)

Holding: "Affirming finding of unconstitutional heat, requiring provisions of fans, ice water, and daily showers when heat index reaches 90 degrees or higher."

At Danville I quoted this case and law in a grievance. Now there is a fan in every segregation cell there.

Now let us address one common misunderstanding in the prisoner body in Illinois. Constitutional law is interpreted by a federal judge. When one district judge rules differently from another district court ruling, one must appeal to the U.S. Court of Appeals seeking a consistent and unified rule. For the Constitution can only be interpreted in one way for all districts. Thus, one must take a case to the U.S. Supreme Court when the appeals courts are in dispute. The U.S. Supreme Court is the big dog that settles all disputes in the United States district and appeals courts.

Illinois is under the Seventh Circuit Court of Appeals located in Chicago, Illinois.

Seventh Circuit Court of Appeal
U.S. Courthouse
219 South Dearborn Street
Chicago, IL 60604

There are three district sections in Illinois—northern, central and southern. It depends on which county your prison is located as to where to file your claim. These can be found in your facilities law library.

Now let us get back to your adequate and correct housing and shelter.

VENTILATION

You have the right to breathe fresh air in your cell. The men and women housed in the maximum security joints face the worse housing here, for they have no window in their cell to open, no way to generate a fresh stream of air. So read the law here, and use it to survive your sentence.

Henderson-vs-DeRobertis, 940 F.2d 1055, 1059 (7th Cir. 1991)

Holding: A prisoner's constitutional right do not come and go with the weather.

Board-vs-Farnham, 394 F. 3d 469, 486 (7th Cir. 2005) Holding:

Holding: "That evidence of the ventilation system being clogged with fiber-glass dust and mold supported an Eight Amendment claim."

Keenan-vs-Hall, 83 F 3d 1083, 1090 (9th Cir. 1996)

Holding: "Claims that the ventilation system was saturated with fumes of feces, urine, and vomit states an Eight Amendment claim." So when the odor from an area other than your cell is harmful and coming in your cell you have a claim.

HEAT

See the previously cited case of

Gates-vs-Cook, 376 F.3d 323, 339-40 (5th Cir. 2004).

Wilson-vs-Seiter, 501 U.S. 304, 111, S. Ct. 2321 (1991)

Holding: "Warmth is a basic need. As low temperatures and no blankets would violate the Eight Amendment and state a claim.

Dixon-vs-Godinez, 114 F. 3d 640, 642-45 (7th Cir. 1997)

Holding:"Convicts have a right to protection from extreme cold. Cold alone may violate the Eight Amendment.

LIGHTING IN THE CELL

The cell is required to have adequate lighting so one may read, do school work and to read and prepare legal documents. At the same time, the prison staff may not use the "count light" (the light the staff turns on at night to do the nightly body count) to deprive the prisoner of the ability to get adequate sleep. The general rule is the light is to be turned off once the correctional officer has taken count and left the wing. This type of sleep deprivation torture has long been recognized and outlawed by the United States Supreme Court.

Adequate lighting must meet the bare minimum of watts to be legal. Most courts set this at 60 watts minimum in the cell. Most count lights are 60 watts bulbs. See:

French-vs-Owens, 777 F.2d 1250, 1252-53 (7th Cir. 1985)

Hoptowit-vs-Spellmen, 753 F.2d 779, 783 (9th Cir. 1985)

Holding: Light inadequate for reading was unconstitutional.

When the staff leave the count light on once the C/O has completed his count and left the deck, this states a claim of cruel and unusual punishment. For there is no penological reason for the light to remain on once the officer has left. If there is a second count required, the control booth officer may simply press the control button and re-light the deck.

Keenan-vs-Hall, 83 F.3d at 1090 (9th Cir. 1996)

Holding: "There is no legitimate penological justification for requiring prisoners to suffer the physical and psychological harm caused by living in constant lighting in the cell. This practice is unconstitutional."

Shepard-vs-Ault, 982 F. Supp. 643, 647-48 (N.D. Iowa 1997)

Holding: "The claim of the 60 watt bulb being on in the cell for 24 hours a day stated a claim. The act of leaving this light on for a period of 283 days and then 550 nights was so far removed from natural sleeping conditions it stated on Eight Amendment violation claims."

In Shepard-vs-Ault the court noted that "The effectiveness of sleep deprivation as a tool of torture has long been recognized and banned by the U.S. Supreme Court. They cited this case then."

Reck-vs-Peck, 367 U.S. 433, 81 S. Ct. 1541 (1961)

Now for some reason the Illinois Department of Corrections staff at the medium facilities believe they may leave the light on in segregation. This is also an illegal act of torture and well recognized in these Federal Cases.

Lemaire-vs-Maass, 745 F. Supp 623, 636 (D.Or. 1993)
at 12 f.2d 1444 (9th Cir. 1993)

Holding: "That keeping the cell light on 24 hours a day in segregation cells is unconstitutional."

So there you have the law and blueprints for filing a meaningful grievance. As prisoner we are sent to prison as punishment, but not to be further punished by the acts of sadistic and abusive staff.

NOISE

Yes, you have the right to sleep in an environment where you are not awakened every few minutes by loud noise. Excessive noise inflicts pain and suffering without legitimate penological interest. For when you cannot sleep your body cannot regenate and heal. Thus it starts to break down physically and mentally. These cases back that interpretation of the cruel-and-unusual-punishment standard found in the U.S. Constitutional Eight Amendment.

Toussaint-vs-McCarthy, 801 F.2d 1080, 1110 (9th Cir. 1986)

Holding: "Allegations that excessive noise occurred every night, often all night long, which deprived the plaintiff of sleep. Thus stating a constitutional claim here."

Benjamin-vs-Fraser, 161 F. Supp. 2d 151, 185 (S.D.N.Y. 2001)

Holding that excessive noise from Diesel generators near housing area where noise was in excess of 45 decibels to 70 decibels nightly stated an Eight Amendment claim."

Remember to file your grievance through all three steps:

The Counselor
The Grievance Officer
The Administrative Review Board

You must state the dates, times and cause of the noise.

CHAPTER NINE

RECREATION & EXERCISE

When a prisoner is placed in the State Penal system, the bare minimum of out-of-cell exercise time is set at five hours per week. This is another basic human right under the Eighth Amendment to the U.S. Constitution. It is there to keep your body fit, not deteriorate while being housed in a cell where you cannot keep physically fit.

Delaney-vs-DeTella, 256 F.3d 679, 683 (7th Cir. 2001)

Wilson-vs-Seiter, 501 U.S. 294, 304, 111 S. Ct. 2321 (1991)

Even the prisoner sent to segregation, or held on lockdown status, must be given access to yard and exercise. The above cited case law addresses this issue. In *Delaney-vs-DeTella*, the court acknowledged this very fact, citing the strong likelihood of psychological and physical injury to a prisoner who was denied access to yard for a period of more than ninety days.

The law is a constant body that evolves with each new challenge brought by prisoner cases. If you are being disruptive in segregation, and it is your fault you keep getting tickets, you have no claim. But under the new standards set in the Civil Rights case for the mentally handicapped, new legal standards were set down. See *Rasho-vs-Walker, U.S.D.C. (C.D. Ill.) Case no. 1:07-cv-01298-MMM*. The standard to protect the mentally ill was finally developed in this case. The prisoner now diagnosed as SMI (severely mentally ill), must be given separate housing and care. They can no longer be given segregation time as a means to house and deal with their mental disorder. If you suffer from mental illness look up your rights here, and enforce them through exposure of your housing conditions and the mental health service care.

For the average convict in general population the following cases apply to your out-of-cell exercise rights.

Davenport-vs-DeRobortis, 844, F.2d 1310, 1315 (7th Cir. 1988)

Pierce-vs-County of Orange, 526 F. 3d 1190, 1212 (9th Cir. 2008)

Holding that requirement of a least two hours per week for pre-trial detainees was required, and would be upheld. But the court did state that most courts set the standard at five to seven hours minimum per week. 129 S.Ct. 597 (2008)

Morales Feliciano-vs-Hernandez Colon, 697 F. Supp. 37, 50 (D.P.R. 1988)

Holding that three hours twice a week was minimum active physical recreation required for the prisoner.

Fogle-vs-Pierson, 435 F.3d 1252, 1260 (10th Cir. 2006)

Hearns-vs-Terhune, 413 F.3d 1036, 1042-43 (9th Cir. 2005)

If you should come upon the situation where the prison staff and schedule requires you to make a choice between exercise and yard or the law library, or commissary, this case also has legal precedence. For a prisoner cannot be required to make a choice between one or the other on a weekly basis.

Allen-vs-City & County of Honolulu, 39 F.3d 936, 939-40 (9th Cir. 1994)

Holding: " Prisoner was entitled to both yard and law library. Could not be forced to take one and forego the other."

Thomas-vs-Ramos, 130 F.3d 754, 764 (7th Cir. 1997)

So you have the right to stay healthy and survive your prison sentence. You need to be be out of your cell to accomplish this.

CHAPTER TEN

SHOWERS ON LOCKDOWN

I write this short chapter for the men and women who serve their time in the maximum security prison. The long lockdowns, for incidents you had no part in, weigh heavy on your basic right to keep clean. A shower is a basic human right under the standard of our society. Clean bodies are a requirement in prison too.

Preston-vs-Thompson, 589 F.2d 300, 308 (7th Cir. 1978)

Holding, "that showers are required to be given twice a week in general population on lockdown status." Once the prison staff has recovered control, and the security threat is over, with the prison body being locked down, these rights kick in.

In general population, at all maximum security facilities, the law is clear on the basic right to three showers a week when off lockdown status.

Walker-vs-Mintzes, 771 F.2d 920, 928-29 (6th Cir. 1985)

Now one case went as far as to require showers every other day in lockdown status. So use the law to get your basic human rights. It all starts with the correct grievance stating the law.

Jefferson-vs-Southworth, 447 F. Supp. 179, 191 (D.R.I. 1978)

Noting "Showers every other day required on lockdown."

Only when you state your rights and grieve the situation will the respect be given to you. Like the guys from Chicago always tell me, "A closed mouth does not get fed." To request your rights through a grievance is a First Amendment-protected right.

CHAPTER ELEVEN

LOST GOOD TIME CREDITS ON A USC 1983 CLAIM

Many a prisoner has made the mistake of filing a 42 U.S.C. § 1983 Civil Rights lawsuit over a bogus ticket—a ticket that is falsely written, for retaliation. But there is a Catch 22 here. If the adjustment committee takes any good conduct credits from the prisoner, he must recover these credits, yes, get them back, before he can pursue a case for justice on the illegal punishment. Some case law states that the prisoner may waive the right to pursue these lost credits. Then he or she may proceed to file and be heard.

If your case has a situation where the lost good conduct credits have not been restored, you will face problems. The state attorney general will move for dismissal. His office will cite the following case and ask that your petition be dismissed with prejudice. Sometimes the court will allow this. But if you file a motion to allow it to be refiled upon getting the restoration, it will preserve your claim to be refiled. See this case:

Heck-vs-Humphrey, 512 U.S. 477, 486-87, 114 S. Ct. 2364 (1994)

Holding that in order to recover damages for allegedly unconstitutional conviction or imprisonment, or for other harm caused by actions whose unlawfulness would render a conviction or sentence has been reversed on direct appeal, or expunged by executive order, declared invalid by a State Tribunal authorized to make such a determination, or called into question by a Federal Court's issuance of a Writ of Habeas Corpus."

Expungement by executive order means the Director of the Department of Corrections has restored your lost good time credits and your out date has not changed. If not the state prisoner must file a state mandamus (a court order seeking that a state official grant a right given by law and due by that official), or a civil court claim to get the ticket overturned and the good time returned. Or file a federal habeas corpus petition (requiring the official to appear before the judge presiding over that judicial district) first to address and recover the lost good time credit.

A prisoner may submit a request to the prison counselor, or adjustment committee, every ninety days to get the lost good time restored by the director. To proceed without having this obstacle to deal with one can skin this cat another way. In most courts the *Heck-vs-Humphrey* ruling will apply and the lost good time credits not being restored will bar civil action. But the prisoner bringing the 1983 Civil Rights complaint may waive the right to recover this lost good time in writing. Then the court may allow him or her to pursue action under this cause.

> *Peralta-vs-Vasquez, 467 F.3d 98 (2nd Cir. 2006)* at
> Key Notes 4 and 5.

Key Note 4, Civil Rights Key 1092: when a prisoner's challenge to a disciplinary hearing involves a sanction that affects only his conditions of confinement, and not his term of confinement, the prisoner may maintain an action under § 1983 without showing, as required by the favorable termination rule, that the sanction, or the procedures that led to it, had been previously invalidated." 42 U.S.C.A. § 1983.

Key Note 5, Civil Rights Key 1092: a prisoner subjected to a single disciplinary proceeding that gave rise to sanctions that affected both the duration of his imprisonment and the conditions of his confinement may, without satisfying the favorite termination requirement that the challenged disciplinary proceedings or resulting punishment have been invalidated, maintain a § 1983 action challenging the sanctions of proceedings affecting the conditions of confinement, but the prisoner may only bring such action if he agrees to abandon forever any and all claims he has with respect to the sanctions that affected the length of his imprisonment. 42 U.S.C.A. § 1983."

So let us break this down for understanding. If under the *Peralta-vs-Vasquez* case you sign a waiver in writing that you are not seeking to recover the good conduct credits taken by the adjustment committee, you may proceed to be heard on the illegal segregation time and disciplinary transfer to harsher conditions of confinement.

Now the prisoner who has illegally been sent to a maximum security prison can seek return to a medium or minimum prison setting; and he may seek damages for the illegal ticket and segregation time. If you were written a ticket and transferred because of your grievance filed at a prison, this is the law. Normally, the federal court will side with the state attorney general. That will require the restoration of the good time lost before you can sue. But under *Peralta-vs-Vasquez* you have an option to this scenario.

REFUSAL TO ANSWER YOUR GRIEVANCE

What to do when the counselor, warden, grievance officer or administrative review board will not answer your grievance?

Yes, every prisoner must exhaust his or her grievance procedure. You must have copies to submit to the court. It must be attached to your original claim filed. Now the rules apply to both sides here, but the prisoner must be diligent in his or her requesting an answer to the grievance once it is filed. I suggest the prisoner keep a written record. Make copies of every letter you send to the counselor, grievance officer or warden. So lets review the steps again once you have filed your grievance.

Counselor: He has fourteen days to respond to your grievance. The counselor will delay. Then after sixty days he will state that they never received the grievance and that you have defaulted by not filing in a timely manner.

So are you going to be played like that? This is the paper trail you will be required to present and prove up in a federal court of law. Go back and review Magistrate Judge William's interpretations of the law (20 Ill. Administrative Code § 504.810 (a).)

Once you have a paper trail where the counselor refuses to answer, the coin is flipped here. Now they have procedural default too. For the state is required to answer in a timely manner also. The court has long been aware of these illegal tactics to stop you from completing the process. See this unpublished case that is the real deal.

> *John Moro-vs-Angela Winsor, 2008 WL 718687*
> *Case No. 05-cv-452-JPG SD OF Ill. March 14, 2008.*

In this case the counselor at the Taylorville Correctional Center refused to answer the grievance. The initial grievance was filed on the religious practice policy in place. Then Moro filed a second set of grievances on the correctional staff that would not answer his grievance. He sent letters and kept copies of these letters, all the way up to the warden.

When John Moro went to the federal court for review the Illinois attorney general screamed foul, trying to get a dismissal stating John Moro had failed to exhaust his administrative remedies. But John was ready for the challenge. At the Pavey hearing (see Chapter Thirteen) the district court judge, Judge Gilbert, quoted the law. For it is in this unpublished case that the Illinois Department of Corrections does not want you to learn the law. So let us review it. (And there are many other cases to back it up.)

"A review of the record reveals that plaintiff initiated a grievance on October 12, 2004. (Doc. 1-1, pp. 10-11). That grievance pertained to all of the issues raised in the complaint and amended complaint. It is not disputed that Plaintiff submitted that grievance to his counselor. (See Doc. 102, p.9; and Doc. 48 p.4). According to the Plaintiff he never received a response from the counselor. In January 2005, plaintiff initiated a grievance regarding the counselor's failure to respond to the October 12, 2004, grievance. (Doc. 1-2, p.12) On February 5, 2005, plaintiff wrote a letter to Warden Walker indicating plaintiff's counselor and a grievance officer had stated that Plaintiff's October 12, 2004 grievance would not be answered, and that his grievance about not getting a response to the grievance had also gone unanswered. (Doc. 1-2, p.7) According to Plaintiff's affidavit, he eventually sent his October 12, 2004 grievance directly to the Administrative Review Board. (Doc. 53-2, p.2) The Administrative Review Board received Plaintiff's October 12, 2004, grievance on May 4, 2005, and immediately returned it without any action because it had not been timely submitted in accordance with Department Rule 504. (Doc. 1-2, p.8; and Doc. 53-2, p.2)."

So you see here how John Moro lay down the paper trail to trap the state employee who deliberately denied him the right and chance to meet the legal requirements on exhausting one's grievance—a smart move that will protect you from a dismissal at a Pavey hearing sought by the Illinois attorney general's office. Prisoner Moro won his case. After he proved up—that the State stopped him from exhausting his grievance—he settled the case. The

Court stated: "Plaintiff appears to have been put in, as he put it, a Catch 22 situation. An inmate must exhaust only those administrative remedies that are available to him." See: 42 U.S.C. § 1997 (e); *Lewis-vs-Washington 300 F.3d 829, 835 (7th Cir. 2002); Johnson-vs-Litscher, 260 F.3d 826, 829 (7th Cir. 2001).*

The Seventh Circuit Court of Appeals holds that "Administrative Remedies" [are] exhausted when prison officials fail to respond to inmate grievances because those remedies had become "unavailable." See *Brengetty-vs-Horton, 423 F.3d 674, 682 (7th Cir. 2005*) (citing *Lewis-vs-Washington, 300 F.3d 829, 835 (7th Cir. 2002*) Holding "we refuse to interpret the PLRA so narrowly as to...permit [prison officials] to exploit the exhaustion requirements through indefinite delay in responding to grievances."

Here, plaintiff alleges that he did not receive a response to either of the grievance he filed, which prevented his ability to pursue his grievance through the formal process. Therefore, it appears the formal administrative remedies were unavailable. At a minimum, a question of material facts exists regarding whether plaintiff exhausted his administrative remedies, and summary judgment is, therefore, not appropriate.

John Moro would go on to win his case. Why? Because he proved that the state employees deliberately refused to answer his grievances.

> *Moro-vs-Winsor Not reported in Feb. Supp 2d 2008 WL 718687 (SD Ill.)*

Holding: For the afore stated reasons, it is this Court's recommendation that Defendant's Gregory Lambert, Roger Walker Jr., Julie Wilkerson and Angela Winsor's Motion For Summary Judgment (Doc. 47) be denied. SD Ill.

Here are more cases holding this ruling—a number of cases that have determined that if you do not get an answer at the initial state to your grievance filed, at whatever required stage, that you have exhausted your remedies by state default.

Boyd-vs-Corr. Corp. of America, 380 F. 3d 989, 996 (6th Cir. 2004)

*Brookins-vs-Vogel, 2006 WL 3437482 *3 (E.D. Cal. Nov. 28, 2006)*

Lane-vs-Doan, 207 F. Supp. 2d 212 (W.D.N.Y. 2003)

So do not fall into this trap. Do not let the State Employee subvert the system. Do not let the issue slid. At every step you must keep a record of your request for an answer.

RESTORATION OF LOST GOOD TIME CREDITS

Once you have exhausted your grievance to get your good conduct credits back, you are not done. You have several steps left. Every prisoner in the Illinois Department of Corrections has the right to be submitted for restoration of lost credits every ninety days, but only the director of the IDOC can deny the restoration of good conduct credits lost. If he denies it, you must get a written reason why.

At some prisons you must write to the adjustment committee chairperson to start the process. At others it is done through your counselor. So ask and then get the process started at the institution.

So let us review the most common abuse of the law in the prisons. If the counselor, the grievance officer,or the adjustment committee chairperson denies you at the institutional level, this is an illegal act. In Illinois, the law states that only the director of the Department of Corrections may revoke and restore lost good time credits. The director must state in writing why he is denying the restoration. You must be given a copy of his response. See: *Hynes-vs-Snyder, 291 Il. Dec. 221, 823 N.E. 2d 231 (Ill. App.2 Dist. 2005).*

Mike Hynes filed a mandamus petition seeking to require Director Donald Snyder to restore his lost good conduct credits. (A mandamus petition is an extraordinary writ issued from a court to an official, compelling the performance of a ministerial act that the law recognizes as an absolute duty.) He sought a factual basis for the director's previous refusal to restore the lost credits.

So let us review the law here. For we live in a house of law, and they work in a house of law. But neither side is above the law. "[11] As required, we begin with the language of the statute. The language of Section 3-5-1(b) is, in relevant part, as follows: 'If the Department * * * makes a determination under this Code which affects the length of the period of confinement, or commitment, the committed person and his counsel shall be advised of factual information relied upon by the Department * * * to make the determination * * *'" 730 ILCS 3-5-1(b) (West 2002).

"In conclusion, we hold that, when the director of the IDOC decides whether to restore good-conduct credits, section 3-5-1(b) requires the director to provide a factual basis for that decision. Thus, in seeking mandamus to compel the production of that information, Hynes has stated a claim upon which relieve can be granted."

In summary, only the director of the IDOC can hear your request for restoration of llost good-conduct credits. He then decides yes or no. If a no is received, a written answer asy to why must by given by the director. No one else holds this power.

CHAPTER TWELVE
WRITING A GRIEVANCE

So let us walk through the grievance form one more time—let us do this one step at a time.

Date: The date you are writing the grievance.

Name: Your full legal name you are incarcerated under.

I.D. #: Your institutional I.D. number on your I.D.

NATURE OF THE GRIEVANCE:

Check the proper box that applies to your issue. If it is a Disciplinary Ticket you go to the line for this. It is best to place the ticket # and C/O who wrote the ticket here also. Then there is no confusion as to what you are grieving about.

If it is an emergency grievance, you complete the section where it requires your signature, providing your number and the date you are signing it. You are required to check the box below the "Relief Requested" section. In Illinois, this sends the grievance straight to the chief administrative officer or warden.

Then state the legal statute, or rule, you are grieving, for example Eight Amendment U.S. Constitution cruel and unusual punishment.

Clothing Issue.

No lights in the cell.

Inadequate housing.

Food. (Diet is making you ill. Not enough.
Not enough time to eat. Losing weight. Etc.)

Theft of property.

Assault by staff or prisoner.

Failure to provide the basic human necessities(such as showers, yards, access to law library, commissary, out-of-cell exercise, cleaning supplies, chance to clean living quarters once a week, laundry.

FICTIONAL EXAMPLE OF A GRIEVANCE

DATE: January 1, 2013

NAME: Joe Convict #0071/2

PLACE WHERE IT HAPPENED: Lawrence Correctional Center. (Current facility is Menard.)

BOX: Other [X] Retaliation for First Amendment Activity

NATURE OF GRIEVANCE: Violation of First Amendment to the U.S. Constitution. Retaliatory transfer to Maximum Security Housing over the lawsuits filed on the staff; not giving me enough time to eat in the chow hall at the Lawrence Correctional Center. See *Rutherford-vs-Pitchess, 457 F. Supp. 104, 116 (C.D.Cal. 1978).*

On the date of June 14th, 2013, I was transferred from the Lawrence Medium Prison to the Menard Maximum Security Prison. I did not receive a ticket,, and this was not a disciplinary transfer. As I have a pending legal action against staff at the Lawrence Prison, there is no other explanation for this transfer. Warden Smiley had me transferred to deter my lawsuit activity.

Retaliation for filing a grievance and civil suit is illegal. See these cases now presented.

Gomez-vs-Randle, 680 F.3d 859 (7th Cir. 2012)

Bridges-vs-Gilbert, 557 F.3d 541,551 (7th Cir. 2009)

To transfer me from a medium security facility to a maximum security facility over my First Amendment activity is illegal. To subject me to harsher conditions of confinement in retaliation is illegal. See the following case law:

King-vs-Zamiara, 2013 WL 2102655 WD Michigan SD
Case # 4:02-cv-141 may 14, 2013

Zimemrman-vs-Tribble, 226 F.3d 568 (7th Cir. 2000)

Higgason-vs-Farley, 83 F.3d 807 (7th Cir. 1996)

Buise-vs-Hudkins, 584 F.2d 223 (7th Cir. 1978)

As I have a basic human right to adequate time to eat in the prison dining room, I filed a grievance and then a civil rights complaint. Once I did this, I was transferred without any reason given. There is no other basis for this transfer to harsher conditions of confinement, except to deter my First Amendment activity. I want the attached list of property taken returned.

RELIEF REQUESTED: I want an immediate transfer back to a medium facility. I want all the property taken from me returned upon transfer. FINAL THOUGHTS

This is the proper way to file a grievance, to start the paper trail toward a civil rights claim. For there is no doubt as to your claim here, who is involved, how it happened and how your rights were violated. Then provide the law supporting your position.

I hope my book helps you get positive results. But sometimes the state employee is just too stubborn to admit you are right. When you need the federal or state court to get justice, it is time to get the 4th Edition of the *Prisoner's Self-Help Litigation Manual.* For information on that book, track down *Prison Legal News Magazine* or you can purchase it from Amazon.com.

Good luck!

CHAPTER THIRTEEN
A PAVEY HEARING

When a prisoner files a lawsuit, the State will always file an answer stating that the prisoner has not exhausted his state remedies. This meant that you have not completed all three steps of the grievance procedure and your case should be dismissed on this technicality.

For under the 1996 Prison Litigation Reform Act, all prisoners are required to do this before they can seek redress in a federal court of law. Each prisoner is required to give the State a chance to remedy this point in the grievance. In Illinois there are the three step: counselor; grievance officer; Administrative Review Board.

PAVEY-vs-CONLEY, 544 F.3d 739, 740-41 (7th Cir. 2008) is the case that set the pattern for a hearing to only develop the facts about the prisoner not exhausting his grievance process. Here you will be able to argue the facts behind your grievance situation.

Here is where you show the facts to the judge. If you have been unable to complete the three steps, it is in this hearing that the judge will state that the state employees failed to allow you to exhaust the grievance process. Thus, your case moves on.

If you fail to prove this, your case will be dismissed. You may request the right to refile your case after the grievance situation has been resolved correctly. This will be up to the judge to dismiss without prejudice, meaning you can re-file.

If the judge states that the case is dismissed *with* prejudice, it is over. The State has won the day and you are done. You can never get heard on the grievance and the issues raised in your petition filed.

So protect yourself! Take the time to lay the paper trail. Fight to exhaust all three steps, for no prisoner may bring a claim to the state or federal curt seeking compensation and changes in policy without completing the three steps: counselor; grievance officer; Administrative Review Board.

A copy of these three steps must be attached to your 42 U.S.C. § 1983 Civil Suit filed, or the state court action taken. If not, then you must prove up why you were denied these grievance steps—when, where and by whom.

So, I hope my book helps you understand the correct steps here. Good luck my fellow prisoners!

ABOUT THE AUTHOR

Larry "Rocky" Harris is serving a sixty-five year sentence for crimes he did not commit. While in prison, he has learned the law. He taught himself how to write legal briefs and respond to the people in power. He has won a few battles in court and helped release some men home to their families. He has fought for better conditions and fairer treatment for those incarcerated. For these efforts, he has often been the subject of abuse and retribution, including solitary confinement and loss of privileges. Larry's life has meaning in his fight for a better penal system, where convicted men and women can be rehabilitated and the poor have access to competent legal defense.

Larry's address can be found be found on the Illinois Department of Corrections website (https://www2.illinois.gov/idoc/Offender/Pages/InmateSearch.aspx), by looking up Larry Harris N-57672.

For updates on prison life, visit his blog at freelarryrockyharrisx2.com.

Made in the USA
Monee, IL
08 November 2026

67971942R00059